Individual Competence Baseline Reference Guide

Individual Competence Baseline

Reference Guide
ICB4 for PMO

Van Haren
PUBLISHING

Colofon

Title:	Individual Competence Baseline Reference Guide ICB4 for PMO
Editorial team:	Bert Hedeman
	Wil Hendrickx
	Ruben Mels
	Jan Willem Velema
	Gert-Jan van de Vrie
Graphical Design:	Based on a design by Dana Kowal:
	Iza Maciejak
Publisher:	Van Haren Publishing, 's-Hertogenbosch, www.vanharen.net
Edition:	Version 1.0
ISBN Hard copy:	978-94-01811-52-1
ISBN eBook:	978-94-01811-53-8
ISBN ePub:	978-94-01811-54-5

© Van Haren Publishing, 2024.

Table of Contents

Foreword

The project management profession has been developing for many years with the world changing. IPMA, as an international organisation with more than 70 national associations develops competence standards that are applied worldwide. IPMA pays great attention not only to project managers but also to all individuals involved in project activities.

Within many years we have developed the standards for individuals, teams and organisations. IPMA ICB (Individual Competence Baseline) is the core competence standard in IPMA and defines the areas of competences – Perspective, People, Practice, Key Competence Indicators (KCIs) and measures of each of the KCIs. Based on IPMA ICB the special Reference Guides have been developed and offered by IPMA worldwide – ICB CCT for Consultants, Coaches and Trainers in project management, Agile Leadership for people working in agile environment, IPMA PEB – Project Excellence Baseline for the project and programme teams, IPMA REB – Research Evaluation Baseline for those who are interested and/or are involved into research activities in project management and IPMA OCB – Organisational Competence Baseline for the organisations and their TOP management.

Today we are glad to introduce a new standard – IPMA ICB Reference Guide for PMO. This standard is dedicated to the structures that support projects, programmes and portfolios to run them effectively and efficiently. These structures are called PMO – Project Management Offices.

A PMO is defined as an organisational unit responsible for the administrative and specialists' support of the responsible management in their management of a (set of) project(s), programme(s) or portfolio(s). PMO plays a very important role in designing, performing, monitoring and reporting activities. Specialists are working in PMO together with the Head of PMO who is leading the unit towards its goals and objectives.

The new standard defines the competences for the individuals working in PMO. All the competences are aligned with the IPMA ICB that is used by all the project, programme or portfolio managers in their everyday activities.

IPMA Reference Guide ICB for PMO will be useful for the professionals who work in PMO, for project, programme or portfolio managers, for the TOP managers as well as HR people for recruiting, assessing and developing personnel in the organisations. It is also good to have this standard as a tool for certification of the individuals working in PMO.

IPMA defines four levels of competence for the individuals working in PMO:
IPMA Level A – Certified PMO Director
IPMA Level B – Certified PMO Senior Manager
IPMA Level C – Certified PMO Manager
IPMA Level D - Certified PMO Specialist

We warmly thank the team members from the Netherlands who developed this standard, and the associations that have been sounding, piloting and approving the IPMA Reference Guide ICB for PMO. We believe that this standard will help professionals all over the world to achieve great results in their projects, programmes and portfolios by using the standard in their everyday lives.

Oxana Klimenko

IPMA Vice President
for Standards and Certification

Joop Schefferlie

IPMA President

Introduction

Internationally, there has been a lot of focus on Project Management Offices (PMO) for several years now. In this context, a PMO is an acronym and stands for Project Management Office, Originally this was a department that sets and maintains project management standards for an organisation. Today, the term PMO is also used for entities responsible for supporting a project, programme or portfolio. Within ICB4, the meaning of PMO and accreditation for PMO practitioners is based on the latter definition.

A PMO is now defined as an organisational unit responsible for the administrative and specialist support of the responsible management in their management of a (set of) project(s), programme(s) or portfolio(s). In this respect, a PMO can be a temporary role but also a permanent position and can range from a single person in one location to several hundred people spread across multiple locations, multiple organisational units and even multiple continents. Finally, the PMO's service portfolio can vary: from support on a single management aspect, e.g. only change management, to support on all management aspects of the responsible management.

Main PMO activities

A PMO has three main activities:

- Design - the creation, establishment and maintenance of standards, processes, procedures and tools that define how work should be done inside.

- Perform - performing administrative and specialist support work.

- Monitoring and reporting - this may involve recording and reporting on the progress of work but also ensuring that agreed arrangements are met. Within all three main activities, the PMO worker also has an advisory role towards their manager and other stakeholders.

Positions of a PMO

Essentially, we recognise four positions of a PMO:

1. Within 'management by projects': as a knowledge centre, the PMO is responsible for the standards with associated templates applicable for the implementation of projects and programmes. It also makes PMO staff available for deployment in projects and programmes. This can be done by seconding them into the projects and/or programmes, but it can also be done from within the project office itself. Often it is a combination of both.

2. Within a portfolio: the PMO is then a permanent entity that supports the portfolio manager in managing the portfolio: helping to select the right projects and programmes, ensuring that these initiatives are implemented according to the standards, reporting on their progress to the portfolio manager, and reporting on the realisation of the intended benefits. Often, such a PMO also includes a knowledge centre responsible for the standards with associated templates applicable to the execution of projects and programmes.

3. Within a programme: the PMO supports the programme manager in the day-to-day management of the programme and fulfils an assurance role to the individual projects within the programme. Within this responsibility, the PMO also acts as a knowledge centre for the projects within the programme.

4. Within a project: The PMO is responsible for providing administrative and specialist support to the project manager for the day-to-day management of the project.

The PMO comes under many names, ranging from project, programme and portfolio office, all depending on the specific function of the PMO in question.

How to demonstrate competent support

IPMA's Individual Competence Baseline version 4 (ICB4) describes the competences required for individuals working in project. programme, and/or portfolio management. In doing so, the ICB4 distinguishes three competence areas: Perspective, People and Practice. Each area contains a number of competence elements. Each competency element (CE) contains the knowledge and skills needed to master the CE. Key Competence Indicators (CIPs) describe the indicators for successful support. Critical Performance Indicators (CPIs) describe within each CIP, the key performance indicators to measure the performance of the CPI.

This reference guide describes the various competency elements for a PMO employee or PMO manager.

In describing these, this Reference Guide refers to projects. This can be read as project, programme and portfolio.

When referring to the 'organisation', this can refer to both the relevant parent organisation(s) and the sponsoring organisation(s) such as for the project the parent programme or portfolio and for the programme the parent portfolio.

A PMO can make an essential contribution to improving organisational competence for managing projects, programmes and portfolios in organisations. See also IPMA's Organisational Competence Baseline (OCB) for this.

Perspective competencies

Context 1. Strategy

Purpose
The purpose of this competence element is to enable the individual to understand the strategy and strategic processes, thus enabling a certain management domain (project, programme or portfolio), to manage the project within the contextual aspects.

Description
Within projects, the PMO can play an important role in ensuring the correlation between the strategy and strategic processes and the project. This concerns both in contributing in aligning the project with the organisation's mission and vision and in identifying opportunities to improve the strategy. Furthermore, they can play a role in preparing the formal investment justification, establishing and maintaining strategic performance management, and monitoring and reporting on critical success factors and performance indicators. From this role, PMO also regularly reflects on the project objectives, identifies risks and opportunities that may affect the strategy and makes proposals to further improve alignment with the organisation's mission, vision and strategy.

Knowledge
- Benefits realisation management;
- Critical success factors;
- Key performance indicators;
- Organisational mission;
- Organisational vision;
- Difference between tactic and strategy;
- Diagnostic and interactive control management systems;
- Strategic performance management;
- Benchmarking;
- Management control systems;
- Strategic schools of thought.

- Analysis and synthesis;
- Entrepreneurship;
- Reflection of the organisation's goals;
- Strategic thinking;
- Sustainable thinking;
- Contextual awareness;
- Result orientation.

Key competence indicators

Context 1.1. Align with organisational mission and vision

- Reflects the mission and vision of the organisation;
- Aligns the project goals with the mission, vision and strategy by using diagnostic control management systems (top-down approach and pre-set goals);
- Controls whether the project's objectives and benefits are in sync with the mission, vision and strategy;
- Develops and implements measures of strategic alignment (e.g. critical success factors, key performance indicators, etc);
- Checks whether the project's organisation is delivering benefits to the organisation.

Context 1.2. Identify and exploit opportunities to influence organisational strategy

- Knows the strategy-making process;
- Identifies new risks and opportunities which could alter the strategy;
- Engages co-workers in questioning the organisational strategy by implementing interactive control management systems (bottom-up approach and stretch goals);
- Identifies strategic improvements;
- Influences the strategy-making process by suggesting changes to strategy.

Context 1.3. Develop and ensure the ongoing validity of the business / organisational justification

- Reflects and defines the business and/or organisational justification;
- Identifies objectives needed in a project to generate the planned benefits; Validates and sells the business and/or organisation justification to the sponsors and/or owners of the projects;
- Re-assesses and validates the justification within the higher context;
- Defines and manages the project configuration (the integral completeness and functionality of the project organisation);

- Applies benefits realisation management to check whether the project configuration is generating the desired results;
- Scans to determine whether there is a need to terminate the project because of redundancy or obsolete strategic importance and change the configuration.

Context 1.4. Determine, assess and review critical success factors
- Derives and/or develops a set of critical success factors (CSFs) for the strategic objectives;
- Uses formal CSFs for strategic alignment, but also identifies their informal context;
- Involves subordinates to question the organisation strategy while developing CSFs (interactive management control – stretch goals);
- Uses the CSFs for strategic alignment of or within a project;
- Uses the CSFs for managing stakeholders;
- Uses the CSFs for developing incentives/rewards and a motivated culture;
- Re-assesses CSF realisation within the higher strategic context.

Context 1.5. Determine, assess and review key performance indicators
- Derives and/or develops a KPI (or set of KPIs) for each critical success factor;
- Decides on the use of leading, lagging and real-time measures when developing KPIs;
- Uses KPIs for managing strategic performance;
- Uses KPIs to influence stakeholders;
- Uses KPIs for developing personal development plans;
- Uses KPIs for developing an incentive/reward system;
- Re-assesses project configuration by employing KPIs and performing benefits realisation management.

Context 2. Governance, structures and processes

Purpose
The purpose of this competence element is to enable the individual to effectively participate in and contribute to managing the impact of governance, structures and processes on projects.

Description
The PMO is an important link in translating, implementing and securing the organisation's established structures, systems and processes to the project. This involves both setting up, maintaining and securing such systems within the project itself and using and coordinating with support structures in the permanent organisation such as human resources (HR), finance and control and information technology (IT).

Knowledge
- Basic principles and characteristics of management by projects;
- Basics of portfolio management;
- Basics of programme management;
- Basics of organisational design and development;
- Formal organisation and informal interrelationships of project, programme and portfolio management (staff, line, etc) in the organisation;
- Governance;
- Organisation and business theories.

Skills and abilities
- Leadership;
- Reporting, monitoring and control;
- Communication planning and executing;
- Design thinking.

Key competence indicators

Context 2.1. Know the principles of project management and the way in which they are implemented
- Recognises a project in practice and has a knowledge of project management principles;

- Explains characteristics of a functional, project and matrix-oriented organisation and recognises one in practice;
- Explains and practices the concept of management by projects;
- Perceives and sets up management by projects concepts within the organisation;
- Explains and identifies the current maturity level of an organisation.

Context 2.2. Know and apply the principles of programme management and the way in which they are implemented
- Explains characteristics of a programme (goals, inputs, outputs, outcomes, benefits);
- Explains the concept of programme management.

Context 2.3. Know and apply the principles of portfolio management and the way in which they are implemented
- Explains characteristics of a portfolio -critical success factors (CSFs) and key performance indicators (KPIs);
- Knows the concept of managing a portfolio (organisational structures and processes);
- Successfully communicates within a respective portfolio in order to successfully manage a project.

Context 2.4. Supporting functions
- Knows people, processes and services of supporting functions;
- Uses the project support function of the parent; organisation for efficient support of the project;
- Establishes and maintains relationships with the project supporting function;
- Applies the reporting standards of the parent organisation to the project, using specific tools and methods.

Context 2.5. Align the project with the organisation's decision-making and reporting structures and quality requirements
- Identifies the organisation's routine and special rules for decision-making in cases beyond his or her authority and responsibility;
- Aligns the communication in projects with the needs of the permanent organisation;
- Applies the reporting standards of the parent organisation to the project, using specific tools and methods;
- Applies the organisation's way of quality assurance when setting up a reporting system within the permanent organisation.

Context 2.6. Align the project with human resource processes and functions
- Uses the human resource function for acquiring staff with the required authorities;
- Deals with the boundaries between the temporary organisation and the human resource function;

- Establishes and maintains relationships with the human resource function;
- Uses human resource processes to provide training and individual development.

Context 2.7. Align the project with finance and control processes and functions

- Knows the processes of the finance and control function;
- Distinguishes between the compulsory and optional utilities of the finance and control function;
- Monitors and controls whether rules, guidelines and other financial utilities are effectively and efficiently used in projects to the benefit of the project;
- Communicates and reports the status and trends of financial tasks clearly and objectively.

Context 3. Compliance, standards and regulations

The purpose of this competence element is to enable the individual to contribute to influencing and managing the alignment of the relevant standards and regulations within the permanent organisation; the relevant sources of legislation and the standards and norms of both the organisation and the wider society and to improve the organisation's approach to these areas.

Description
Standards and regulations influence and define the way projects should be organised and managed to be feasible and successful. Standards and regulations cover compliance with requirements related to laws and regulations, contracts and agreements, intellectual property and patents, health, safety, security and environmental protection, and professional standards.

The PMO plays an important role in translating, setting up and managing the relevant standards and regulations to the project. Furthermore, it is ideally placed to regularly assess and challenge compliance within the project. Finally, it can contribute in improving organisational maturity in these areas.

Knowledge
- Law regulation systems involved; Autonomous professional regulation;
- Professional standards and norms, e.g. IPMA standards;
- ISO standards (e.g. ISO21500 guidance on project management or other standards of ISO/TC258);
- Sustainability principles;
- Benchmarking theory;
- Benchmarking tools and methods;
- Knowledge management;
- Codes of ethics;
- Codes of business conduct;
- Differences between law theories.

Skills and abilities
- Critical thinking;
- Benchmarking;
- Adapting standards to specific organisations;

- Communicating standards and regulations;
- Leading by example.

Key competence indicators

Context 3.1. Identify and ensure that the project complies with all relevant legislation
- Acknowledges the legal context and its applications;
- Filters out and uses the relevant law regulation;
- Identifies risks in the regulations in relation to the project and consults the experts;
- Acknowledges and manages the regulatory agencies as stakeholders;
- Aligns procurement routes with the regulations.

Context 3.2. Identify and ensure that the project complies with all relevant health, safety, security and environmental regulations (HSSE)
- Identifies the relevant HSSE regulations for the project;
- Defines the HSSE context for the project;
- Identifies risks arising from implementing HSSE measures to the project;
- Provides a safe, secure and healthy environment for the project team members;
- Applies HSSE for project sustainability.

Context 3.3. Identify and ensure that the project complies with all relevant codes of conduct and professional regulation
- Knows the appropriate codes of business conduct;
- Knows the appropriate professional regulation for the particular industry sector (public administration, civil engineering, information technology, telecommunication, etc);
- Identifies ethics principles;
- Identifies and uses the tacit trading laws not set by the code;
- Aligns procurement practices with the codes of business conduct;
- Works to prevent violation of the code by the project team members.

Context 3.4. Identify and ensure that the project complies with relevant sustainability principles and objectives
- Identifies the social and environmental consequences of the project;
- Defines and communicates the sustainability targets for the project and its outcomes;
- Aligns objectives with organisational strategy for sustainability;
- Balances the demands of society, the environment and the economy (people, planet, profit) with project processes and products;
- Encourages the development and diffusion of environmentally friendly technologies.

Context 3.5. Assess, use and develop professional standards and tools for the project

- Identifies and uses the relevant professional standards;
- Identifies the specifics of a standard and manages the risks arising from applying a standard to a project;
- Identifies and uses the best practice for managing a project;
- Develops and implements custom-made standards for managing project team members.

Context 3.6. Assess, benchmark and improve the organisational project management competence

- Identifies and assesses the relevant deficient areas of organisational competence in project management;
- Identifies and sets relevant benchmarks for the deficient areas;
- Identifies the benchmarking baseline and best practice;
- Benchmarks current performance against best practice;
- Identifies measures for the needed improvements;
- Implements the identified measures and assesses the benefits gained;
- Disseminates the acquired know-how throughout the project organisation.

Context 4. Power and interest

Purpose
The purpose of this competence element is to enable the individual to use power and interest techniques to contribute to stakeholder satisfaction and deliver the agreed outcomes within the constraints of time and budget.

Description
Since the PMO has a support function within the project, it is eminently important for them to understand the personal ambitions, influence and interests of others and their potential impact on the project but also to use them to the project's benefit wherever possible. The personality and behaviour of those involved also play an important role in this. If necessary, the PMO worker himself will also have to be able to use power and authority to secure the project's interests.

Knowledge
- Formal organisation (staff, line, etc) versus informal structures;
- Informal decision-making processes;
- Formal and informal power and influence;
- Difference between power and authority;
- Reach of influence;
- Sources of interests;
- Conformity;
- Bases of power;
- Project psychology;
- Organisational culture and decision-making;
- Power theories.

Skills and abilities
- Observing and analysing psychological processes;
- Recognising and using influence;
- Using power when appropriate;
- Discovering values;
- Revealing stakeholders' interests.

Context 4.1. Assess the personal ambitions and interests of others and the potential impact of these on the project

- Acknowledges and assesses the personal ambitions and interests of relevant people or groups;
- Acknowledges and assesses the differences between personal and organisational interests and goals.

Context 4.2. Assess the informal influence of individuals and groups and its potential impact on the project

- Acknowledges and can estimate the influence, power and reach of certain individuals in various settings;
- Is able to discern group affiliations and relationships in relation to the project.

Context 4.3. Assess the personalities and working styles of others and employ them to the benefit of the project

- Identifies and acknowledges the differences between behavioural style and personality;
- Identifies and acknowledges the differences between cultural aspects and personality.

Context 5. Culture and values

Purpose
The purpose of this competence element is to enable the individual to contribute to recognising and integrating the influence of internal and external cultural aspects on the project approach, objectives, processes, sustainability of the outcomes and agreed outcomes.

Description
Every organisation has its own culture and values. Moreover, every organisation operates in a society, which also has a specific culture and possible subcultures and values. Finally, team members bring their own culture and values shaped by the society they come from. All these cultural aspects and values influence the way individuals interact with each other.

The PMO should be able to recognise the influence of all these aspects on the approach and agreed outcomes of the project, as well as on the collaboration within the project and with third parties, and tailor her services accordingly.

Knowledge
- Relevant cultural traits, values, norms and admissible behaviour;
- Organisational mission and vision;
- Mission statements;
- Corporate values and policies;
- Quality policies;
- Ethics;
- Corporate social responsibility (CSR);
- Green project management;
- Theories about culture.

Skills and abilities
- Values awareness;
- Cultural awareness;
- Respect for other cultures and values;
- Aligning to and working within different cultural environments;
- Dealing with issues related to cultural aspects;
- Bridging different cultures and values to achieve the project, programme or portfolio objectives.

Context 5.1. Assess the culture and values of the society and their implications for the project

- Knows and acknowledges the cultural values, norms and demands of a society;
- Knows, acknowledges and understands the implications of cultural values, norms and demands for the project;
- Works according to societal cultural demands and values without compromising personal values.

Context 5.2. Align the project with the formal culture and corporate values of the organisation

- Acknowledges and respects the organisation's formal norms and demands;
- Knows and applies the organisation's corporate values and mission;
- Knows and applies the quality policy of an organisation;
- Acknowledges the implications of formal norms, demands, corporate values and mission and quality policy for the project;
- Acts sustainably by practising corporate social responsibility.

Context 5.3. Assess the informal culture and values of the organisation and their implications for the project

- Acknowledges, analyses and respects the informal culture and values of the organisation(s);
- Identifies the implications of the organisation's informal culture and values for the project; in conformity with the organisation's informal values and norms.

People competencies

People 1. Self-reflection and self-management

Purpose
The purpose of this competence element is to enable the individual to control and direct his or her behaviour by acknowledging the influence of his or her personal set of emotions, preferences and values. This enables effective and efficient use of the individual's resources and leads to positive work energy and a balance between inside and outside work.

Description
For everyone, it is important to reflect on how one's own values and experiences influence one's work. Furthermore, it is important to identify one's own strengths, weaknesses and limitations, as well as to set personal goals and focus and reflect on them in order to grow personally but also in work.

Within the service role, this is particularly important for a PMO-er to avoid having your work determined solely by what others do not pick up and having your task completion depend entirely on the delusion of the day. Make sure your own work matches what the project needs but also matches your own objectives. Know what you can do and manage work in relationships with others from self-knowledge and self-management.

Knowledge
- Reflection and self-analysis techniques;
- Stress management of self and others;
- Relaxation techniques and methods;
- Pace of work;
- Feedback rules and techniques;
- Prioritisation techniques;
- Personal time management;
- Checks of progress;

- Formulation of objectives (e.g. SMART method);
- Effectiveness theories.

Skills and abilities
- Awareness of own work styles and preferences;
- Awareness of instances that lead to personal distractions;
- Self-reflection and self-analysis;
- Controlling emotions and focusing on tasks, even when provoked;
- Self-motivation; -Delegating tasks;
- Setting meaningful and authentic individual goals;
- Carrying out regular checks of progress and results;
- Dealing with mistakes and failures.

Key competence indicators

People 1.1. Identify and reflect on the ways in which own values and experiences affect the work
- Reflects on own values;
- Uses own values and ideals to shape decisions;
- Communicates own principles and personal demands;
- Expresses and discusses own experience;
- Puts own experience in perspective;
- Uses own experience to build hypotheses about people and situations.

People 1.2. Build self-confidence on the basis of personal strengths and weaknesses
- Identifies own strengths, talents, limits and weaknesses;
- Delivers strengths, talents and passions;
- Identifies solutions to overcoming personal weaknesses and limitations;
- Maintains eye contact even in stressful situations;
- Accepts setbacks without losing confidence.

People 1.3. Identify and reflect on personal motivations to set personal goals and keep focus
- Demonstrates knowledge of own motivations;
- Sets personal and professional goals and priorities;
- Selects actions that contribute to the personal goals;
- Names personal distractors;
- Regularly reflects in order to maintain focus on the goals;
- Delivers personal commitments on time;
- Focuses on tasks despite numerous distractions or interruptions;
- Provides own direction or seeks clarification in uncertain situations.

People 1.4. Organise personal work depending on the situation and own resources

- Keeps record of own time planning;
- Prioritises competing demands;
- Says no when appropriate;
- Engages resources to maximise delivery;
- Adapts language;
- Develops tactics appropriate to the situation.

People 1.5.Take responsibility for personal learning and development

- Uses mistakes or bad results as an impulse for learning activities;
- Uses feedback as a chance for personal development;
- Seeks consultation;
- Measures own performance;
- Focuses on continuous improvement of own work and capacities.

People 2. Personal integrity and reliability

Purpose
The purpose of this competence is to enable the individual to make consistent decisions, take consistent actions and behave consistently in projects. Maintaining personal integrity supports an environment built on trust that makes others feel secure and confident. It enables the individual to support others.

Description
The competence as a PMO to make critical assessments of situations involving conflicting values and norms in order to arrive at morally acceptable actions.
This increasingly involves the sustainability of the approach as the outcome of the action. It is also important to deliver what has been promised on time in order to operate reliably towards third parties. This requires clear agreements to be made within the available capacities, and requires decisiveness, persistence and binding reliable behaviour. Within the PMO's position in the project, these are constant points of attention.

Knowledge
- Codes of ethics/codes of practice;
- Social equity and sustainability principles;
- Personal values and moral standards;
- Ethics;
- Universal rights;
- Sustainability.

Skills and abilities
- Development of confidence and building of relationships;
- Following own standards under pressure and against resistance;
- Correcting and adjusting personal behaviour.

Key competence indicators

People 2.1. Acknowledge and apply ethical values to all decisions and actions
- Knows and reflects own values,
- Uses own values and ideals to shape decisions,
- Communicates own principles.

People 2.2. Promote the sustainability of outputs and outcomes
- Proactively addresses sustainability issues in solutions;
- Considers and incorporates long-term outcomes into the solution.

People 2.3. Take responsibility for own decisions and actions
- Assumes full responsibility for own decisions and actions;
- Demonstrates ownership of both positive and negative results;
- Takes decisions and sticks to agreements established with others;
- Addresses personal and professional shortcomings that get in the way of professional success.

People 2.4. Act, take decisions and communicate in a consistent way
- Demonstrates alignment between words and actions;
- Uses similar approaches to solve similar problems;
- Adjusts personal behaviour to the context of the situation.

People 2.5. Complete tasks thoroughly in order to build confidence with others
- Completes work assignments thoroughly and carefully;
- Earns confidence through the delivery of complete and accurate work.

People 3. Personal communication

Purpose
The purpose of this competence element is to enable the individual to communicate efficiently and effectively in a variety of situations, to different audiences and across different cultures, and to support others in doing so.

Description
In the project, the PMO often has many consultations with many different parties on a wide range of topics. The PMO is also often the spider in the web when it comes to exchanging information between the various parties. It is therefore of the utmost importance that, as a PMO, you communicate clearly but also make sure that what has been communicated is understood and that others feel committed to fulfilling the agreements made. Also indicate how received information will be processed or passed on. In doing so, choose effective communication channels, be alert to all kinds of noise and, if necessary, use humour and other angles to ensure messages are better understood and received.

Knowledge
- Differences between information and message;
- Different methods of communicating;
- Different questioning techniques;
- Feedback rules;
- Facilitation;
- Presentation techniques;
- Communication channels and styles;
- Rhetoric;
- Characteristics of body language;
- Communication technologies.

Skills and abilities
- Use different ways of communicating and different styles for effective communication;
- Active listening;
- Questioning techniques;
- Empathy;
- Presentation and moderation techniques;
- Effective use of body language.

Key competence indicators

People 3.1. Provide clear and structured information to others and verify their understanding
- Structures information logically depending on the audience and the situation;
- Considers using story-telling when appropriate;
- Uses language that is easy to understand;
- Delivers public speaking and presentations;
- Coaches and gives training;
- Leads and facilitates meetings;
- Uses visualisation, body language and intonation to support and emphasise messages.

People 3.2. Facilitate and promote open communication
- Creates an open and respectful atmosphere;
- Listens actively and patiently by confirming what has been heard, re-stating or paraphrasing the speaker's own words and confirming understanding;
- Does not interrupt or start talking while others are talking;
- Is open and shows true interest in new ideas;
- Confirms message/information is understood or, when needed, asks for clarification, examples and/or details;
- Makes clear when, where and how ideas, emotions and opinions are welcome;
- Makes clear how ideas and opinions will be treated.

People 3.3. Choose communication styles and channels to meet the needs of the audience, situation and management level
- Selects appropriate communication channels and style depending on the target audience;
- Communicates via selected channels according to the selected style;
- Monitors and controls communication;
- Changes the communication channels and style depending on the situation.

People 3.4. Communicate effectively with virtual teams
- Uses modern communication technology, (e.g. webinars, tele-conferences, chat, cloud computing);
- Defines and maintains clear communication processes and procedures;
- Promotes cohesion and team building.

People 3.5. Employ humour and sense of perspective when appropriate
- Changes communication perspectives;
- Decreases tension by use of humour.

People 4. Relationships and commitment

Purpose
The purpose of this competence element is to enable the individual to build and maintain personal relationships and to understand that the ability to engage with others is a precondition for collaboration, commitment and, ultimately, performance.

Description
For the PMO-er, it is often not the formal position but personal relationships that are the basis for productive collaboration and the personal involvement and commitment of others. This includes both establishing one-to-one relationships and establishing a whole network of relationships. As a PMO, you need to invest time and attention in building lasting and strong relationships with individuals. The ability to establish strong relationships is mainly driven by social traits such as empathy, trust, self-confidence and communication skills. Sharing visions and goals with individuals and the team encourages others to perform tasks and commit to the common goals. Establishing personal relationships, building a network of relationships and thereby ensuring the involvement and commitment of third parties are essential from the PMO's service role.

Knowledge
- Intrinsic motivation;
- Motivation theories;
- Handling resistance;
- Values, traditions, individual requirements of different cultures;
- Network theory.

Skills and abilities
- Use of humour as icebreaker;
- Appropriate ways of communicating;
- Respectful communication;
- Respecting others and being aware of ethnical and cultural diversity;
- Trusting own intuition.

Key competence indicators

People 4.1. Initiate and develop personal and professional relationships
- Actively seeks possibilities and situations to make new contacts;
- Demonstrates interest in meeting new people;

- Uses humour as an icebreaker;
- Is present, available and open for dialogue;
- Stays actively in contact, establishes a routine for bilateral meetings;
- Keeps others informed.

People 4.2. Build, facilitate and contribute to social networks
- Joins and contributes to social networks;
- Creates and facilitates social networks;
- Organises events for networking;
- Facilitates support for networking.

People 4.3. Demonstrate empathy through listening, understanding and support
- Listens actively;
- Makes others feel heard;
- Asks questions for clarification;
- Relates to the problems of others and offers help;
- Familiarises with the values and standards of others;
- Responds to communication within a reasonable time.

People 4.4. Show confidence and respect by encouraging others to share their opinions or concerns
- Relies on a given word;
- Assigns tasks to team members based on confidence;
- Expects others to act according to common values and agreements;
- Delegates work without monitoring and controlling every single step;
- Asks others for their ideas, wishes and concerns;
- Notices and respects differences between people;
- Embraces the importance of professional and personal variety.

People 4.5. Share own vision and goals in order to gain the engagement and commitment of others
- Acts positively;
- Clearly communicates vision, goals and outcomes;
- Invites debate and critique of the vision, goals and outcomes;
- Involves people in planning and decision-making;
- Asks for commitment on specific tasks;
- Takes individual contributions seriously;
- Emphasises the commitment of all to realise success.

People 5. Leadership

Purpose
The purpose of this competence element is to enable the individual to contribute to leading, providing direction and motivating others in order to enhance individual and team performance.

Description
Leadership involves directing and motivating others in their roles and tasks to achieve goals. From the PMO role, this is often not from a formal position but on the basis of conviction. What is needed and why. This is most effective in personal contact. Offer to help, advise, guide and use influence and persuasion to realise what is needed. Often because of the lack of formal position, it is precisely leadership that is of eminent importance for a PMO-er to function effectively within the bigger picture. Leadership here can relate to the entire project and to the PMO team.

Knowledge
- Leadership models;
- Individual learning;
- Communication techniques;
- Coaching;
- Sense-making and sense-giving;
- Bases of power;
- Decision taking (consensus, democratic/majority, compromise, authority, etc).

Skills and abilities
- Personal self-awareness;
- Listening skills;
- Emotional strength;
- Capacity to express a set of values;
- Dealing with mistakes and failure;
- Sharing values;
- Creating team spirit;
- Methods and techniques for communication and leadership;
- Management of virtual teams.

Key competence indicators

People 5.1. Initiate actions and proactively offer help and advice
- Proposes or exerts actions;
- Offers unrequested help or advice;
- Thinks and acts with a future orientation (i.e. one step ahead);
- Balances initiative and risk.

People 5.2. Take ownership and show commitment
- Demonstrates ownership and commitment in behaviour, speech and attitudes;
- Talks about the project in positive terms;
- Rallies and generates enthusiasm for the project;
- Sets up measures and performance indicators;
- Looks for ways to improve the project processes;
- Drives learning.

People 5.3. Provide direction, coaching and mentoring to guide and improve the work of individuals and teams
- Provides direction for people and teams;
- Coaches and mentors team members to improve their capabilities;
- Establishes a vision and values and leads according to these principles;
- Aligns individual objectives with common objectives and describes the way to achieve them.

People 5.4. Exert appropriate power and influence over others to achieve the goals
- Uses various means of exerting influence and power;
- Demonstrates timely use of influence and/or power;
- Perceived by stakeholders as the leader of the project or team.

People 5.5. Make, enforce and review decisions
- Deals with uncertainty;
- Invites opinion and discussion prior to decision-making in a timely and appropriate fashion;
- Explains the rationale for decisions;
- Influences decisions of stakeholders by offering analyses and interpretations;
- Communicates the decision and intent clearly;
- Reviews decisions and changes decisions according to new facts;
- Reflects on past situations to improve decision processes.

People 6. Teamwork

Purpose
The purpose of this competence element is to enable the individual to contribute to selecting the right team members, promote a team orientation and effectively manage a team.

Description
Teamwork is about building a productive team by effectively forming, supporting and leading the team. Team communication and team relations are among the most important aspects of successful teamwork. As a PMO, you often contribute emphatically to the selection of the project team, the cooperation within the team and the effective management of the team. You also contribute to team development and to empowering the team by facilitating the delegation of tasks and responsibilities to individual team members and to the team as a whole... As a PMO manager, you lead the building and development of a PMO team. The PMO team members (as a collective) must have all the knowledge, skills and capabilities to achieve the team's goal.

Knowledge
- Project organisation;
- Team role models;
- Team lifecycle models.

Skills and abilities
- Recruiting and personnel selection skills;
- Interview techniques;
- Building and maintaining relationships;
- Team building;
- Facilitation skills.

Key competence indicators

People 6.1. Select and build the team
- Considers individual competences, strengths, weaknesses and motivation when deciding on team inclusion, roles and tasks;
- Clarifies objectives and creates a common vision;
- Sets the team objectives, agenda and completion criteria;
- Negotiates common team norms and rules;
- Motivates individuals and builds team awareness.

People 6.2. Promote cooperation and networking between team members
- Creates opportunities for team member discussions;
- Asks for opinions, suggestions and concerns from team members in order to improve performance;
- Shares successes with the team(s);
- Promotes cooperation with people both within and outside the team;
- Takes appropriate action when team cooperation is threatened;
- Uses tools for collaboration.

People 6.3. Support, facilitate and review the development of the team and its members
- Promotes continuous learning and knowledge sharing;
- Uses techniques to engage in development e.g. on-the-job training;
- Provides opportunities for seminars and workshops (on-and off-the-job);
- Plans and promotes 'lessons learned' sessions;
- Provides time and opportunity for self-development of team members.

People 6.4. Empower teams by delegating tasks and responsibilities
- Delegates tasks when and where appropriate;
- Empowers people and teams by delegating responsibility;
- Clarifies performance criteria and expectations;
- Provides reporting structures at team level;
- Provides individual and team feedback sessions.

People 6.5. Recognise errors to facilitate learning from mistakes
- As far as possible, avoids negative effects of errors on project success;
- Realises that mistakes happen and accepts that people make mistakes;
- Shows tolerance for mistakes;
- Analyses and discusses mistakes to determine improvements in processes;
- Helps team members to learn from their mistakes.

People 7. Conflict and crisis

Purpose
The purpose of this competence element is to enable the individual to take effective actions when a crisis or clash of opposing interests/incompatible personalities occurs.

Description
Conflicts can arise within one's own PMO team, between team members within the project and in their collaboration with other teams and stakeholders. A PMO officer, in his role as a supporter of the project manager, can identify potential conflicts and crisis early and, from that role, can also play a facilitating role to prevent conflicts from escalating.

Anticipate conflicts and crises and try to prevent them if possible. Analyse the causes and consequences of conflicts. Mediate the resolution of conflicts and crises and/or their consequences. Learn from what happened share this with others to improve future practices.

Knowledge
- De-escalation techniques;
- Creativity techniques;
- Moderation techniques;
- Scenario techniques;
- Conflict stage models;
- Value of conflicts in team building;
- Crisis plan;
- Worst case scenarios.

Skills and abilities
- Diplomatic skills;
- Negotiation skills, finding a compromise;
- Moderation skills;
- Persuasiveness;
- Rhetorical skills;
- Analytical skills;
- Stress resistance.

Key competence indicators

People 7.1. Anticipate and possibly prevent conflicts and crises
- Analyses potentially stressful situations;
- Keeps conflicting characters or interests in separate tasks/teams;
- Delegates conflict-sensitive items to specific people;
- Implements preventive measures;
- Takes stress-reducing measures;
- Reflects on stressful situations in a team.

People 7.2. Analyse the causes and consequences of conflicts and crises and select appropriate response(s)
- Assesses conflict stage;
- Analyses causes of a conflict or crisis;
- Analyses potential impact of a conflict or crisis;
- Has different conflict or crisis approaches available to choose from.

People 7.3. Mediate and resolve conflicts and crises and/or their impact
- Addresses issues openly;
- Creates an atmosphere of constructive debate;
- Selects and uses the right method to solve the conflict or crisis;
- Takes disciplinary or legal measures when appropriate.

People 7.4. Identify and share learning from conflicts and crises in order to improve future practice
- Restores the team environment;
- Motivates the team to acknowledge and learn from their own part in the conflict;
- Uses conflicts in a positive way to progress;
- Strengthens the team cohesion and solidity with regard to potential future conflicts and crises.

People 8. Resourcefulness

Purpose

The purpose of this competence element is to enable the individual to effectively handle uncertainty, problems, changes, limitations and stressful situations by systematically and continuously searching for new, better and more effective approaches and/or solutions, and to support others in doing so.

Description

The PMO contributes to resourcefulness in the project by acquiring and deploying effective resources that promote creativity within the team but also by ensuring that unnecessary administrative tools and techniques are not deployed that hinder resourcefulness within the team.

The PMO also promotes an attitude of resourcefulness within the team by fostering a safe environment where people can experiment and share ideas, without negative judgement from others. Finally, the PMO can contribute to the use of creativity techniques, such as the use of workshops, to find solutions to the problems that arise.

Knowledge

- Techniques to solicit views of others;
- Conceptual thinking;
- Abstraction techniques;
- Strategic thinking methods;
- Analytic techniques;
- Convergent and divergent thinking;
- Creativity methods;
- Innovation processes and techniques;
- Coping methods;
- Lateral thinking;
- Systems thinking;
- Synergy and holistic thinking;
- Scenario analysis;
- SWOT technique;
- PESTLE analysis;
- Creativity theories;
- Brainstorming techniques e.g. lateral thinking;
- Converging techniques (comparative analysis, interview techniques).

Skills and abilities

- Analytical skills;
- Facilitating discussions and group working sessions;
- Choosing appropriate methods and techniques to communicate information;
- Thinking 'outside the box' – new ways of doing things;
- Imagining an unknown future state;
- Being resilient;
- Dealing with mistakes and failure;
- Identifying and seeing different perspectives.

Key competence indicators

People 8.1. Stimulate and support an open and creative environment

- Encourages people to share their knowledge and contribute their opinions;
- Stimulates and supports creativity when appropriate;
- Uses and stimulates original and imaginative ways to overcome obstacles;
- Seeks input from others and shows willingness to consider and/or adopt their ideas;
- Considers the perspectives of others.

People 8.2. Apply conceptual thinking to define situations and strategies

- Uses or promotes conceptual thinking when appropriate;
- Knows that problems often have multiple causes and that solutions often have multiple effects;
- Applies systemic thinking.

People 8.3. Apply analytic techniques to analysing situations, financial and organisational data and trends

- Applies various analytic techniques;
- Analyses problems to detect causes and possible solutions;
- Analyses complex sets of data and extracts relevant information;
- Clearly reports and presents data conclusions, summaries and trends.

People 8.4. Promote and apply creative techniques to find alternatives and solutions

- Uses creative techniques when appropriate;
- Applies diverging techniques;
- Applies converging techniques;
- Engages multiple views and skills;
- Identifies interdependencies.

People 8.5. Promote a holistic view of the project and its context to improve decision-making

- Demonstrates holistic thinking and an can explain the bigger picture;
- Uses multiple perspectives to analyse and deal with the current situation;
- Makes connections between the project and the larger context and takes appropriate action.

People 9. Negotiation

Purpose
The purpose of this competence element is to enable the individual to reach satisfactory agreements with others by using negotiation technique.

Description
From the position of a PMO, the PMO-er has to negotiate with many parties on a wide range of issues. This often involves not official institutionalised negotiations but reaching agreement on the deployment and application of resources, the approach to be chosen, the distribution of resources, the application of certain values and principles and the realisation of targets. This both within the team and with stakeholders inside and outside the organisation. In this way, the PMO facilitates the project manager is his role as leader of the team and manager of the project.

Knowledge
- Negotiation theories;
- Negotiation techniques;
- Negotiation tactics;
- Phases in negotiations;
- BATNA (best alternative to a negotiated agreement);
- Contract templates and types;
- Legal and regulatory provisions associated with contracts and agreements;
- Analysis of cultural aspects and tactics.

Skills and abilities
- Identification of the desired outcomes;
- Assertiveness and drive to reach desired outcomes;
- Empathy;
- Patience;
- Persuasion;
- Establishing and maintaining trust and positive working relationships.

Key competence indicators

People 9.1. Identify and analyse the interests of all parties involved in the negotiation
- Knows and reflects own interests, needs and constraints;
- Gathers and documents relevant hard and soft information about interests, needs and expectations of all parties involved;
- Analyses and documents available information to identify own priorities and likely priorities for other parties.

People 9.2. Develop and evaluate options and alternatives with the potential to meet the needs of all parties
- Identifies trade-offs, options and alternative solutions based on the analysis of interests, needs and priorities of all parties;
- Proposes the right option at the right time in the right way.

People 9.3. Define a negotiation strategy in line with own objectives that is acceptable to all parties involved
- Identifies possible negotiation strategies in order to achieve the desired outcome;
- Identifies secondary strategies and alternative options to address 'what if' scenarios;
- Selects a negotiation strategy and can explain why it has been chosen;
- Analyses and selects negotiation techniques and tactics to support the desired negotiation strategy;
- Identifies key parties to participate in the negotiation and clearly articulates their mandate.

People 9.4. Reach negotiated agreements with other parties that are in line with own objectives
- Negotiates using techniques and tactics appropriate to the circumstances to achieve the desired outcome;
- Negotiates to achieve a sustainable agreement;
- Demonstrates patience and drive to realise a sustainable agreement;
- Implements BATNA if a sustainable outcome is not possible;
- Documents the outcomes of the negotiation.

People 9.5. Detect and exploit additional selling and acquisition opportunities
- Seeks ways to deliver the agreed outcomes sooner, better and/or cheaper;
- Weighs alternatives to the current situation and agreements;
- Considers the impact of alternatives on current relationships.

People 10. Results orientation

Purpose
The purpose of this competence element is to enable the individual to focus on the agreed outcomes and drive towards making the project a success.

Description
A results-oriented approach is important within every project. Results must be delivered, with which the organisation wants to achieve its goals. To achieve that result, acting efficiently and effectively is a prerequisite.

The PMO plays a crucial role in this when, from the hectic pace of the day, the end result is sometimes lost from sight and people and resources are not deployed effectively. By communicating the progress and intermediate results achieved, a careful change procedure, but also constant attention to avoid waste, overload and irregularities, the PMO can make a significant contribution to the result orientation of the project as a whole.

Knowledge
* Organisation theories;
* Efficiency principles;
* Effectiveness principles;
* Productivity principles.

Skills and abilities
* Delegation;
* Efficiency, effectiveness and productivity;
* Entrepreneurship;
* Integration of social, technical and environmental aspects;
* Sensitivity to organisational do's and don'ts;
* Management of expectations;
* Identifying and assessing alternative options;
* Combining helicopter view and attention to essential details;
* Total benefit analysis.

Key competence indicators

People 10.1. Evaluate all decisions and actions against their impact on project success and the objectives of the organisation
- Considers the objectives and agreed outcomes of the project as leading all actions;
- Formulates own goals based on the objectives and outcomes;
- Derives the strategy of the project from the goals;
- Judges all decisions and actions by their impact on the success of the project.

People 10.2. Balance needs and means to optimise outcomes and success
- Assesses and prioritises various needs;
- Explains why certain actions get more priority;
- Uses the results orientation as a means to say 'no' (and explain why).

People 10.3. Create and maintain a healthy, safe and productive working environment
- Shields the team from outside interference;
- Creates healthy, safe and stable working conditions;
- Provides a clear set of work on which team members can operate;
- Provides the necessary resources and infrastructure.

People 10.4. Promote and 'sell' the project, its processes and outcomes
- Defends and promotes the objectives, approach, processes and agreed outcomes;
- Seeks openings and venues to promote the project;
- Invites others to join in with marketing the project.

People 10.5. Deliver results and get acceptance
- Differentiates the concepts of efficiency, effectiveness and productivity;
- Plans and sustains planned levels of efficiency, effectiveness and productivity;
- Demonstrates the ability to get things done;
- Focuses on and shows continuous improvement;
- Thinks in solutions, not in problems;
- Overcomes resistance;
- Recognises limitations to getting results and addresses these shortcomings.

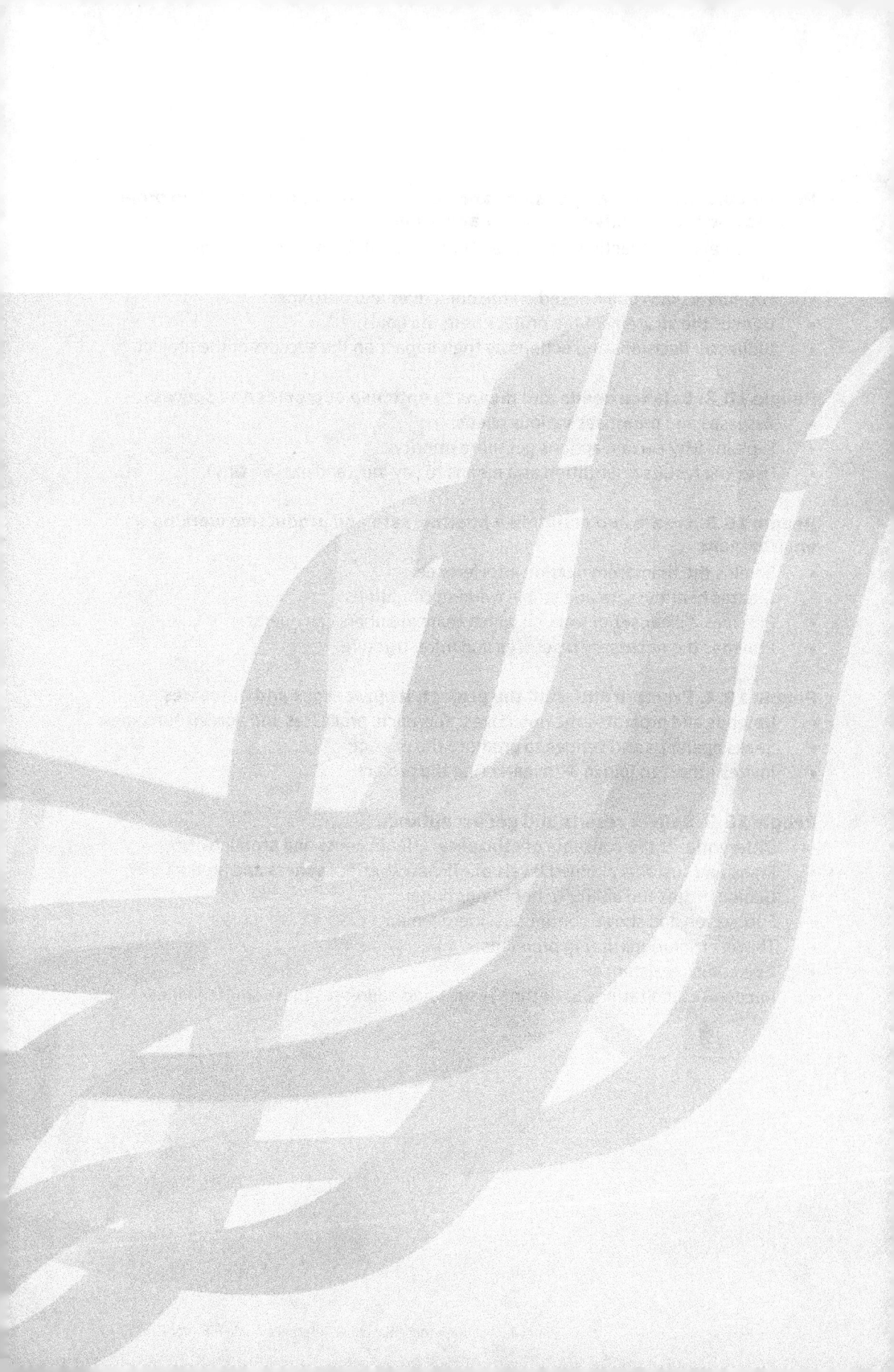

Practice competencies

Practice 1. Project design

Purpose

The purpose of this competence element is to enable the individual to contribute to the successful integration of all contextual and social aspects and derive the most advantageous approach for a project to ensure buy-in and success.

Description

As PMO, you play a crucial role in selecting the right project approach, as well as in recognising, prioritising and reviewing success criteria. You provide guidelines and templates for formulating measurable and realistic success criteria. Throughout the project, you will monitor progress and performance against these success criteria and conduct regular reviews to ensure they are still relevant and achievable. You support in assessing the complexity of the project and understand its potential impact on the project approach. You work with the project team and other stakeholders to understand the impact of complexity on the project and determine what adjustments are needed in the project approach. It is also important to be open to and use experiences and learning points from previous projects for the purpose of establishing the approach and identifying risks. Recording own experiences and learning points and sharing them with other projects contributes to project success.

Knowledge

- Critical success factors;
- Success criteria;
- Lessons learned;
- Benchmarking;
- Complexity;
- Project, programme and portfolio success;
- Project, programme and portfolio management success;
- Project, programme and portfolio management tools;
- Leadership styles;

- Strategy;
- Triple constraint (iron triangle);
- Performance management;
- Organisation project design rules and methodologies;
- Specific methodologies related to line of business and context;
- Organisational models, e.g. contingency theory;
- Theory of change.

Skills and abilities
- Contextual awareness;
- Systems thinking;
- Result orientation;
- Improvements by/incorporation of lessons learned;
- Structure decomposition;
- Analysis and synthesis.

Key competence indicators

Practice 1.1. Acknowledge, prioritise and review success criteria
- Identifies, classifies, evaluates and prioritises influences from each of the five perspective aspects relevant for success;
- Recognises and assesses both formal and informal influencing elements;
- Evaluates and prioritises success criteria from each of the five contextual aspects;
- Acknowledges and assesses both formal and informal success criteria;
- Acknowledges and uses relevant success factors;
- Performs periodic re-assessments of the relevance of success criteria;
- Performs periodic re-assessments of the relevance of success factors.

Practice 1.2. Review, apply and exchange lessons learned from and with other projects
- Acknowledges and gathers lessons learned from previous projects;
- Applies relevant lessons learned;
- Acknowledges and uses research and benchmarking methods for improving the performance of the project;
- Identifies and shares lessons learned from the project with the organisation.

Practice 1.3. Determine complexity and its consequences for the approach
- Identifies the level of complexity of the project by applying appropriate methods;
- Acknowledges complexity-enhancing aspects;
- Identifies and defines the impact on complexity of specific processes, constraints or outcomes;

- Identifies and assesses the impact on complexity of specific external and internal parameters;
- Assesses and applies complexity-diminishing measures.

Practice 1.4. Select and review the overall project management approach
- Assesses and appraises various possible approaches;
- Selects an approach for the project that has the highest chance of leading to success;
- Explains and defends the chosen approach and its relation to the success of the
- project;
- Explains the main effects of the chosen approach on the organisation of the project;
- Explains the main effects of the chosen approach on the parent organisation;
- Periodically re-evaluates the chosen approach based on contextual and internal developments;
- Makes necessary changes to the approach and explains why these were made.

Practice 1.5. Design the project execution architecture
- Establishes the project execution architecture with outcomes;
- Defines the business rules and control philosophy;
- Monitors the project against the architecture components;
- Updates the architecture based on changes.

Practice 2. Requirements and objectives

Purpose

The purpose of this competence element is to enable the individual to contribute to establishing the relationship between what stakeholders want to achieve and what the project is going to accomplish.

Description

As a PMO, you help define and develop the goal hierarchy. For example, by providing a structured approach to identify, clarify and prioritise goals, taking into account the organisation's strategic objectives. You play an active role in identifying and analysing stakeholder needs and requirements and to identify key stakeholders and understand their needs. As a PMO, you also play an important advisory role in prioritising and making decisions regarding requirements and acceptance criteria. For example, you will help define a structured process for prioritising requirements based on their urgency, importance and impact on the project, and provide guidelines and templates to support stakeholders in defining clear and measurable acceptance criteria for validating deliverables

Knowledge

- Temporary and permanent organisation;
- Expectations, needs and requirements;
- Project charter;
- Project sponsor (owner);
- Fit for use, fit for purpose;
- Value management;
- Acceptance criteria;
- Benefits mapping;
- Goal analysis;
- Strategy setting.

Skills and abilities

- Corporate strategy;
- Stakeholder relationships;
- Knowledge elicitation;
- Workshop facilitation;
- Interviewing;
- Formulation of objectives (e.g. SMART methodology);
- Synthesis and prioritisation.

Practice 2.1. Define and develop the project goal hierarchy
- Establishes the relationship between the organisational and project goals;
- Establishes the relationship between the project goals and objectives;
- Defines a goal hierarchy for the project;
- Explains the relevance and content of the goal hierarchy.

Practice 2.2. Identify and analyse the project stakeholder needs and requirements
- Knows the difference between need, expectations and requirements;
- Identifies and documents stakeholder needs and requirements;
- Establishes the structures for traceability of deliverables back to requirements;
- Analyses stakeholder needs and requirements.

Practice 2.3. Prioritise and decide on requirements and acceptance criteria
- Prioritises stakeholder needs and requirements;
- Documents and agrees on stakeholder needs and requirements;
- Supports and oversees the translation of requirements into acceptance criteria.

Practice 3. Scope

Purpose

The purpose of this competence element is to enable the individual to contribute to acquiring insight into what the boundaries of the project scope are, to manage this scope and to understand how scope influences (and is influenced by) decisions regarding the management and execution of the project.

Description

As a PMO, you will support in identifying and defining deliverables. This includes analysing the objectives and translating them into tangible results that the project should deliver, or the benefits expected from a programme. You play an active role in defining and managing the scope. It is vital to delineate the scope and ensure that it is realistic and achievable. As a PMO, you help identify the required work, resources and time schedule needed to achieve the objectives. In addition, you support the project in identifying, defining and structuring work packages. You establish a detailed work package structure, breaking down the objectives into smaller, manageable units. You monitor the progress of work packages, contributing to effective and efficient implementation.

Knowledge

- Configuration management;
- Hierarchical and non-hierarchical structures;
- Planning packages;
- Scope definition (with exclusions);
- Scope gathering methodologies, e.g. use case scenarios, history writing;
- Scope creep;
- Constraints;
- Deliverable design and control methods;
- Work breakdown structure (WBS);
- Product breakdown structure (PBS);
- Work packages;
- WBS dictionary.

Skills and abilities

- Scope configuration;
- Prioritisation;
- Defining a WBS;
- Defining a PBS;

- Using a WBS dictionary;
- Agile development. Key competence indicators

Practice 3.1. Define the project deliverables
- Defines the project deliverables;
- Knows and explains the difference between goals and deliverables;
- Organises the goals and the associated deliverable(s);
- Knows and uses the goal hierarchy and its purpose.

Practice 3.2. Structure the project scope
- Knows and explains the purpose and benefits of a scope defining structure;
- Knows and applies the principles for creating the WBS;
- Explains the differences between different principles of the WBS;
- Explains the characteristics of project boundaries and can give examples;
- Argues for why and when a full WBS may be inappropriate with an iterative (agile) approach to the project.

Practice 3.3. Define the work packages of the project
- Defines work and planning packages;
- Explains the purpose and benefits of (well) defined work packages;
- Names and explains ways to define a work package.

Practice 3.4. Establish and maintain scope configuration
- Manages the scope configuration;
- Defines roles and responsibilities related to scope configuration management;
- Relates the dependency of scope configuration and the overall approach to the
- project (sequential or iterative);
- Compares progress and earned value against a baseline plan.

Practice 4. Time

Purpose

The purpose of this competence element is to enable the individual to contribute to defining, sequencing, optimising, monitoring and controlling all components necessary to delivering the agreed outcomes of the project.

Description

Time schedules are essential for planning and controlling a project. As a PMO, you play a crucial role in achieving time planning and phasing in projects. You support the project team in identifying and establishing all activities required to deliver the project and in estimating the labour effort and duration of activities. You advise in decisionmaking on the project's time planning and phase approach. You will help analyse different planning scenarios and identify potential risks and dependencies. As a PMO-er, you also provide guidance on setting milestones and determining the optimal phasing of the project. In addition, as a PMO-er, you are responsible for monitoring the progress of the project against the time plan. You regularly report on the status of the schedule to the project team and stakeholders. If deviations are identified, you assist in analysing the causes and suggesting possible corrective measures. You ensure that the schedule is updated and advise on making necessary adjustments to manage any delays and ensure that the project stays on schedule.

Knowledge

- Planning types;
- Estimation methods;
- Levelling;
- Scheduling methods (e.g. Gantt chart, Kanban charts);
- Resource allocation;
- Network analysis;
- Baselines;
- Critical path planning;
- Crashing the schedule;
- Time boxing;
- Phases;
- Milestones;
- Fast modelling and prototyping;
- Spiral/iterative/agile development process.

- Define activities from work packages;
- Define dependencies;
- Sequence components;
- Estimate activity resources and duration.

Practice 4.1. Establish the activities required to deliver the project

- Defines activities related to the realisation of project deliverables;
- Extracts activities from a WBS work package.

Practice 4.2. Determine the work effort and duration of activities

- Determines work effort and duration of activities;
- Identifies types of resources that may be required to perform an activity;
- Identifies and decides between various resource options.

Practice 4.3. Decide on schedule and stage approach

- Knows different planning techniques;
- Chooses the appropriate planning techniques;
- Determines appropriate stages;
- Knows the effects of uncertainty on planning; and what to do to minimise the effects.

Practice 4.4. Sequence project activities and create a schedule

- Sequences a series of project activities;
- Determines dependencies and dependent relationships;
- Calculates the critical path;
- Levels resource assignment for a given plan.

Practice 4.5. Monitor progress against the schedule and make any necessary adjustments

- Knows when and how to use various schedule control systems;
- Applies planning adjustments in response to various types of disturbances;
- Compares progress and earned value against a baseline plan.

Practice 5. Organisation and information

Purpose

The purpose of this competence element is to enable the individual to contribute to creating a high-performing temporary organisation, which also includes the inseparable link between organisational structure and communication processes.

Description

As a PMO, you play a key role in effectively managing information and documentation within a project. You will be responsible for establishing the structure, roles and responsibilities related to information and documentation within the project. This includes identifying the various stakeholders involved in managing information and documentation. You create clarity on who is responsible for managing, creating, updating, distributing and archiving information and documentation. You develop procedures and guidelines for creating, storing, sharing and securing documents, as well as managing version control and access rights. From your role, you will monitor compliance with documentation requirements and ensure quality control so that project information remains consistent, accurate and accessible throughout the project lifecycle.

Knowledge

- Organisational models;
- WBS as a base for project organisation;
- Document management systems;
- Information and documentation systems;
- Information plan;
- Regulatory requirements;
- Information security;
- Ways to organise governance for projects and programmes.

Skills and abilities

- Involve/convince others;
- Staffing of organisation;
- Task delegation;
- Management of interfaces to other parts of the organisation;
- Dealing with project software tools in the office;
- Preparation techniques for official documents;
- Information management planning.

Practice 5.1. Assess and determine the needs of stakeholders relating to information and documentation
- Assesses and documents the information and documentation needs of the project;
- Establishes various modes of communication, including formal and informal;
- Determines the project characteristics influencing the organisational needs.

Practice 5.2. Define the structure, roles and responsibilities within the project
- Explains some fundamental ways to structure a temporary organisation;
- Designs and develops a governance framework and structure;
- Defines the responsibilities of the various key personnel on the project;
- Identifies links to and interfaces with corporate governance arrangements;
- Identifies and records the differences between the organisation's functional authorities and the project's authorities.

Practice 5.3. Establish infrastructure, processes and systems for information flow
- Explains the purpose and contents of information processes;
- Communicates internal information via various methods;
- Ensures redundant information is limited and/or prevented;
- Explains the benefits of different types of meetings;
- Explains what is covered by an infrastructure for communication;
- Establishes planning and control mechanisms (e.g. documentation of key decisions).

Practice 5.4. Implement, monitor and maintain the organisation of the project
- Implements new organisational structures;
- Monitors the organisation, including the roles involved;
- Adjusts the organisation, including the roles involved.

Practice 6. Quality

Purpose

The purpose of this competence element is to enable the individual to contribute to establishing and managing the quality of the service/product to be delivered and the delivery process being managed; and to recognise quality as an invaluable tool for the benefits realisation management process.

Description

As a PMO officer, you play an important role in monitoring quality in and of a project. You will help draw up and monitor the quality management plan, with responsibility for updating this plan throughout the project. You will regularly review the project and deliverables to ensure that they continue to meet the requirements of the quality management plan. This includes monitoring performance indicators to identify any deviations or shortcomings and suggest corrective actions. Throughout the project, as a PMO, you will ensure quality within the project. This includes implementing quality assurance processes and procedures, ensuring compliance with standards and best practices, and promoting a culture of continuous improvement within the project team.

Knowledge

- Validation and verification;
- Process quality management tools (e.g. Lean, Six Sigma, Kaizen);
- Product quality management;
- Cost of quality;
- Quality management standards (e.g. TQM, EFQM, Theory of Constraints, Deming Cycle);
- Organisational quality analysis tools;
- Standard operating procedures;
- Policies implementation;
- Design for testing;
- Utilising indicators;
- Inspection methods and techniques;
- Risk-based testing;
- Testing techniques, including, for example, automated testing;
- Continuous integration;
- Software application for handling and managing tests and defects.

- Analysing the impact of quality management on projects and people;
- Implementing a standard (process and people);
- Adapting a quality standard;
- Correcting people's and the group's behaviours with a wide variety of interventions;
- Developing and executing quality plans;
- Conducting quality assurance procedures;
- Performing quality audits and interpreting their results;
- Design of test plans.

Key competence indicators

Practice 6.1. Develop and monitor the implementation of and revise a quality management plan for the project

- Develops and monitors a quality plan;
- Names different types of quality objectives;
- Implements measures to achieve defined quality objectives;
- Defines and implements quality measures;
- Explains and names different types of tools/techniques for achieving quality objectives;
- Explains and names procedures for achieving quality objectives;
- Explains how to align the quality management activities to the overall project activities and also refers to own experiences (projects).

Practice 6.2. Review the project and its deliverables to ensure that they continue to meet the requirements of the quality management plan

- Explains different ways of reviewing the project performance and the project processes;
- Names key elements necessary for an effective and efficient project review;
- Explains how to communicate project quality objectives;
- Names different reasons for performing a project audit;
- Performs a quality audit;
- Analyses a quality audit and is able to define measures or change requests;
- Presents at least one example of a corrective action.

Practice 6.3. Verify the achievement of project quality objectives and recommend any necessary corrective and/or preventive actions

- Describes the outcome of a planned and performed verification process referring to own experiences gained on projects;
- Explains the contents and outputs of a root cause analysis carried out on the basis of detected defects;
- Explains the process and goals of peer reviews;

- Performs verification and recommends corrective actions;
- Outlines the contents and steps in communicating preferred and recommended corrective actions and change requests, referring to own experiences gained on projects.

Practice 6.4. Plan and organise the validation of project outcomes
- Explains the difference between verifying and validating;
- Documents different types of quality objectives suitable for quality validation;
- Conducts a validation exercise of project outcomes;
- Obtains a term of acceptance from a client.

Practice 6.5. Ensure quality throughout the project
- Assesses, adapts and integrates quality standards being used by organisations;
- Implements quality processes in the project/programme/portfolio;
- Conducts regular assessments of the implemented processes and improves them when needed
- Implements quality awareness in the project/programme/portfolio, so that everyone involved knows what quality is required;
- Conducts regular assessments of the quality awareness and takes corrective action when needed.

Practice 7. Finance

Purpose

The purpose of this competence element is to enable the individual to contribute to ensuring that enough financial resources are provided to the project at any time, that the financial targets of the project can be met and that the financial status is monitored, reported and properly used for adequate management of financial resources.

Description

As a PMO, you play a crucial role in managing costs and financial needs in projects. When estimating project costs, as a PMO you will support the project team in identifying and quantifying all expected costs, including personnel, materials and external services. You will be responsible for preparing the project budget Securing project funding is also a task of the PMO. You work with stakeholders to secure the required funding, including identifying funding sources, preparing business cases and obtaining approval for the required budget. You continuously monitor project finances to identify and correct deviations from the project plan. As a PMO, you act as a focal point for financial information and reporting, giving project managers and stakeholders insight into the project's financial performance. By performing these roles effectively, as a PMO-er, you will help optimise cost control, budget planning and achieve financial success in projects, programmes or portfolios.

Knowledge

- Financial accounting basics (cash flow, chart of accounts, cost structures);
- Cost estimating methods (e.g. single or multi-expert estimations (*Delphi* method), *historical* data, analogies, effort models, parametric estimations (function point method), three point estimation);
- Cost calculation techniques (e.g. direct, indirect calculation, activity-based costing, etc);
- Design-to-cost/target costing;
- Processes and governance for cost management;
- Methods for monitoring and controlling expenditures;
- Performance indicators (earned value);
- Reporting standards;
- Forecasting methods (linear, parametric, velocity analysis);
- Financing options;
- Funding sources;
- Financial management concepts and terms, such as (but not limited to) cash flow, debt-asset ratio, return on investment, rates of return;
- Contingency approaches;
- Relevant conventions, agreements, legislation and regulations, including (but not

limited to) taxation, currency exchange, bilateral or regional trade agreements, international commercial terms, World Trade Organisation determinations.

Skills and abilities

- Convincing/negotiating with sponsors;
- Scenario techniques;
- Interpreting and communicating the actual cost situation;
- Developing financial forecasts and models;
- Writing skills;
- Presentation skills;
- Reading financial statements;
- Interpreting financial data and identifying trends;
- Financial management approach analysis;
- Developing a project budget;
- Setting frameworks for resource project cost estimation;
- Directing and authoring cost strategies and cost management plans;
- Developing and maintaining cost management systems;
- Conducting analysis, evaluating options and implementing responses to project cost variations.

Key competence indicators

Practice 7.1. Estimate project costs
- Sets up cost structures and identifies cost categories;
- Selects appropriate cost calculation technique (e.g. direct calculation);
- Sets the cost targets by consulting any relevant standards or internal guidelines.

Practice 7.2. Establish the project budget
- Establishes budget plans;
- Develops budget scenarios based on cost-relevant items;
- Plans budget for contingencies;
- Assesses the budget against the time and funding and makes possible adjustments;
- Sets the final budget.

Practice 7.3. Secure project funding
- Establishes funding strategies for projects;
- Identifies sources of funds;
- Handles the organisational approval processes;
- Cooperates, keeps close contact to and can negotiate with potential sponsors in order to get funds.

Practice 7.4. Develop, establish and maintain a financial management and reporting system for the project

- Defines processes and governance for financial management;
- Defines financial performance indicators on the project;
- Relates the project cost structure to the organisational cost structure (e.g. aggregating work packages);
- Develops appropriate reports in accordance with the project's organisation and governance.

Practice 7.5. Monitor project financials in order to identify and correct deviations from the project plan

- Establishes and evaluates cost reports;
- Analyses and interprets financial situations;
- Uses financial performance indicators to monitor and control the project;
- Produces project performance forecasts based upon the financial indicators;
- Signals cost breaches and suggests mitigation plans in accordance with the project's organisation and governance for any cost breaches that cannot be handled by the programme budget contingencies.

Practice 8. Resources

Purpose
The purpose of this competence element is to enable the individual to contribute to ensuring that the resources required are available and assigned as needed in order to meet the objectives.

Description
As a PMO manager, you may be involved in aligning capacity demand, determining overall capacity requirements, acquiring and deploying the required capacity, monitoring and monitoring capacity deployment and performance, and advising and taking corrective action if necessary. The PMO manager is responsible for capacity management within his or her own PMO.

Knowledge
- Resource allocation methods;
- Resource assessment;
- Resource utilisation calculations and collection techniques;
- Competence management;
- Procurement processes, supply and demand concepts;
- Training.

Skills and abilities
- Resource planning, allocation and management;
- Identifying and classifying different ways of working;
- Developing resources skills matrix
- identifying skills and documenting individual skills gaps;
- Prioritising and allocating resources, given multiple competing priorities.

Key competence indicators

Practice 8.1. Develop strategic resource plan to deliver the project
- Identifies project resource requirements based on resource forecasts;
- Captures baseline of existing and proposed resources;
- Reviews and analyses the resource capacity of the organisation and identifies trends;
- Coordinates with constituent organisation or portfolio management processes.

Practice 8.2. Define the quality and quantity of resources required
- Describes the resources needed for the project;
- Draws up a resource plan (based on detailed project planning);
- Defines the amount and quality of the required resources.

Practice 8.3. Identify the potential sources of resources and negotiate their acquisition
- Takes 'make or buy' decisions;
- Creates and evaluates sourcing alternatives;
- Defines a sourcing strategy;
- Engages with resource providers;
- Negotiates resource availability.

Practice 8.4. Allocate and distribute resources according to defined need
- Links resources with project structure;
- Creates schedules (or task lists) for resources;
- Negotiates resource conflicts.

Practice 8.5. Evaluate resource usage and take any necessary corrective actions
- Defines a systematic approach to evaluating the use of resources;
- Provides opportunities to enhance competences/skills;
- Addresses a skill shortage with the relevant team member and his or her line management.

Practice 9. Procurement

Purpose

The purpose of this competence element is to enable the individual to contribute to obtaining the best value possible from the chosen suppliers or partners and thus deliver the best value for the buyer and the organisation.

Description

Project success depends heavily on the availability of people and resources. Procurement and outsourcing are becoming increasingly important in a project, as more and more organisations concentrate on their core business and increasingly use third parties to carry out project.

The PMO can contribute to the entire procurement process; identifying procurement needs, soliciting bids, evaluating and selecting suppliers, and negotiating and agreeing contracts, all in coordination with the responsible manager and procurement department. Finally, the PMO may administratively oversee the correct execution of contracts.

Knowledge

- Sourcing strategies;
- Make/buy analysis;
- Supplier development methodologies;
- Organisational procurement policies, procedures and practices;
- Procurement methods (e.g. RFI, RFP, RFQ);
- Contract types (e.g. firm fixed price, time and materials, cost plus);
- Claim management processes, methods and tools;
- Tender procedures and practices;
- Contractual judicial knowledge;
- Contractual terms and conditions;
- Supply chain management.

Skills and abilities

- Tactical know-how;
- Presentation skills;
- Contract administration.

Practice 9.1. Agree on procurement needs, options and processes
- Defines reasons (based on needs) for procurement or partnership;
- Prepares, produces or collects the necessary information as input to the procurement subject matter experts;
- Defines tender documents and selection criteria based on needs;
- Supports procurement preparation processes and procedures.

Practice 9.2. Contribute to the evaluation and selection of suppliers and partners
- Launches request for quotation (tender), if necessary in cooperation with the procurement function;
- Outlines and defines the various steps in a supplier selection process;
- Defines and explains the contents of tender documents;
- Defines and uses the selection criteria;
- Aligns with formal procurement regulations (international, national and branchspecific);
- Assesses the specifics of the procurement and suggests partnership models (e.g. joint ventures, long-term partnerships, etc).

Practice 9.3. Contribute to the negotiation and agreement of contractual terms and conditions that meet project objectives
- Defines a negotiation mandate and sets objectives to be negotiated;
- Distinguishes different contractual forms and their implications for the project;
- Knows contractual terms and conditions and reflects their implications for the project;
- Negotiates a contract by establishing price, availability and customisation possibilities and procurement schedules.

Practice 9.4. Supervise the execution of contracts, address issues and seek redress where necessary
- Implements measures to manage contract performance;
- Identifies deviations from the contract;
- Handles contractual breaches by taking corrective measures (e.g. talks, renegotiations, etc);
- Involves - in the case of difficulties in renegotiations - legal, logistic and/or procurement functions of the organisation;
- Handles contractual disputes and claims made by the supplier;
- Concludes and ends the agreed business relationship when either the project is in risk or all of the obligations in the contract have been met.

Practice 10. Plan and control

Purpose

The purpose of this competence element is to enable the individual to contribute to establishing and maintaining a balanced and integrated view over the management of a project. Maintaining the balance, consistency and performance is crucial in order to achieve the agreed outcomes.

Description

During the project start-up, the PMO officer is often of great value in drafting the various baselines, such as the project brief and the project management plan; setting up the project administration; agreeing and drafting working procedures and setting up the necessary registers and file structure.

During execution, the PMO officer is indispensable in making estimates, monitoring and reporting on progress, and managing obligation administration and liquidity planning. In addition, the PMO officer is often involved in preparing progress reports and status reports such as the phase-end report.

Finally, the PMO often makes a major contribution to project closure; cleaning up and closing the project administration; preparing the project final report, organising a final evaluation and project closure, administrative handling of the project delivery, handing over the project documents, and dismantling the project facilities.

Knowledge

- Phase/stage transitions;
- Reporting;
- Project office;
- Deming cycle (plan-do-check-act);
- Request for change;
- Management by objectives;
- Management by exception;
- Lessons learned report;
- Phase/stage/sprint/release planning;
- Request for change;
- Decision to fund and make or buy;
- Exception reports;
- Issue reports;
- Project management plan;
- Project (phase) evaluation;

- Discharge;
- Decision-making authority.

- Progress control meetings;
- Change management;
- Reporting;
- Negotiation of change requests;
- Start-up workshop;
- Kick-off meeting;
- Close-out meeting;
- Issue management;
- Change management;
- Earned value analysis;
- Slip charts.

Practice 10.1. Start the project and develop and get agreement on the project management plan

- Organises the project start-up process;
- Gathers all necessary information from the stakeholders and experts;
- Analyses, values and prioritises information;
- Organises and facilitates a project start-up workshop;
- Prepares the project charter or project management plan and gets agreement on it;
- Prepares and communicates the plan for the project management effort;
- Initiates and manages the transition to a new project phase.

Practice 10.2. Initiate and manage the transition to a new project phase

- Organises the management of the project execution process;
- Defines the goals and deliverables of the following phase(s);
- Manages the phase transition;
- Organises and facilitates a kick-off meeting.

Practice 10.3. Control project performance against the project plan and take any necessary remedial actions

- Defines a performance control cycle;
- Describes means and methods applicable for performance control;
- Measures progress and performance.

Practice 10.4. Report on project progress

- Makes a reporting structure (what, when, how often, how, etc);
- Makes a progress report;

- Makes a forecast report;
- Makes phase transition reports.

Practice 10.5. Assess, get agreement on and implement project changes
- Organises a process for managing changes;
- Makes an exception or change report;
- Changes the scope configuration.

Practice 10.6. Close and evaluate a phase or the project
- Organises the project close-out process;
- Organises and facilitates a close-out workshop;
- Facilitates a complete project evaluation;
- Prepares a project 'lessons learned' report.

Practice 11. Risk and opportunity

Purpose
The purpose of this competence element is to enable the individual to contribute to understanding and effectively handling risks and opportunities, including responses and overall strategies.

Description
The PMO can play an important role by drawing up the risk management approach and setting up and maintaining a risk and opportunity register. In addition, from his supporting and monitoring role, the PMO officer can identify risks and opportunities that require management attention, assist in assessing probability and impact, and support in establishing, implementing and monitoring mitigating measures. In addition, the PMO can help ensure that risk management does not degenerate into an administrative task but is an essential tool in proactively managing the project.

Knowledge
- Strategies for managing risk and opportunity;
- Contingency plans, fallback plans;
- Cost and duration contingency reserves;
- Expected monetary value;
- Qualitative risk assessment tools and techniques;
- Quantitative risk assessment tools and techniques;
- Risk and opportunity response strategies and plans;
- Risk identification techniques and tools;
- Scenario planning;
- Sensitivity analysis;
- Strengths, weaknesses, opportunities, threats analysis (SWOT);
- Risk exposure, appetite, aversion and tolerance;
- Project or programme risks and business risks and opportunities;
- Residual risk;
- Risk and opportunity probability, impact and proximity;
- Risk owner;
- Risk register;
- Sources of risk and opportunity.

Skills and abilities
- Risk and opportunity identification techniques;
- Risk and opportunity assessment techniques;
- Developing risk and opportunity response plans;

- Implementing, monitoring and controlling risk and opportunity response plans;
- Implementing, monitoring and controlling overall strategies
- For risk and opportunity management;
- Monte Carlo analysis;
- Decision trees (e.g. Ishikawa analysis).

Key competence indicators

Practice 11.1. Develop and implement a risk management framework
- Identifies a range of potential risk management models;
- Develops a risk management framework consistent with organisational policy and international standards;
- Ensures the consistent application of the risk management framework.

Practice 11.2. Identify risks and opportunities
- Names and explains various sources of risk and opportunity and the differences between them;
- Identifies risks and opportunities;
- Documents risks and opportunities in a register.

Practice 11.3. Assess the probability and impact of risks and opportunities
- Engages in qualitative risk and opportunity assessment;
- Engages in quantitative risk and opportunity assessment;
- Makes and interprets a risk or opportunity decision tree, with outcomes.

Practice 11.4. Select strategies and implement response plans to address risks and opportunities
- Explains various means and methods for implementing a chosen overall strategy for the risk and opportunity management process;
- Evaluates responses to risks and opportunities, including their strengths and weaknesses;
- Evaluates alternative means and methods for implementing a risk and opportunity response plan;
- Influences the plan for resources and competences required to implement responses;
- Implements and communicates a risk and opportunity response plan.

Practice 11.5. Evaluate and monitor risks, opportunities and implemented responses
- Monitors and controls the implementation and execution of a risk and opportunity response plan;
- Communicates the risks and opportunities and the appropriateness of the selected responses.

Practice 12. Stakeholders

Purpose

The purposeof this competence istoenabletheindividual tocontribute to managing stakeholder interests, influence and expectations, to engage stakeholders and effectively manage their expectations.

Description

The PMO-er can contribute to identifying stakeholders and analysing their importance and influence. The PMO can also contribute to developing a stakeholder management strategy and drafting the communication plan, However, from their support and reporting role, the PMO can particularly contribute to engaging stakeholders by operationally involving them in the progress of the project and building networks and alliances within the agreed stakeholder strategy.

Knowledge

- Stakeholder interests;
- Stakeholder influence;
- Engagement strategies;
- Communication plan;
- Collaborative agreements and alliances;
- External environment scanning relating to social, political, economic and techno-logical developments.

Skills and abilities

- Stakeholder analysis;
- Analysis of contextual pressures;
- Demonstrating strategic communication skills;
- Expectations management;
- Formal and informal communication;
- Presentation skills;
- Networking skills to identify potentially useful and opposing stakeholders;
- Contextual awareness;
- Undertaking conflict resolution.

Practice 12.1. Identify stakeholders and analyse their interests and influence
- Identifies the major stakeholder categories;
- Identifies and names various stakeholders' interests;
- Identifies and evaluates stakeholders' influence;
- Identifies relevant changes in or around the project;
- Analyses the consequences of changes for the project;
- Takes actions in order to manage stakeholders.

Practice 12.2. Develop and maintain a stakeholder strategy and communication plan
- Describes the importance of a stakeholder strategy;
- Prepares a communication plan;
- Adjusts the communication plan and/or strategy based on changed circumstances;
- Explains reasons for changing a communication plan;
- Identifies and evaluates opportunities for alliances and partnerships;
- Identifies and evaluates potential collaborators.

Practice 12.3. Engage with the executive, sponsors and higher management to gain commitment and to manage interests and expectations
- Engages management and/or sponsor(s);
- Manages expectations of the project's executive, higher management and/or sponsor(s);
- Employs the executive and/or sponsor(s) to act as ambassadors.

Practice 12.4. Engage with users, partners, suppliers and other stakeholders to gain their cooperation and commitment
- Engages users and commits them to the project;
- Commits suppliers to the project;
- Cooperates with partners to deliver the optimal result for the organisation.

Practice 12.5. Organise and maintain networks and alliances
- Negotiates and documents the alliance agreement;
- Develops and implements a plan for cooperation;
- Develops and evaluates measures for success;
- Maintains key partnership agreements;
- Closes all formal contractual agreements.

Practice 13. Change and transformation

Purpose
The purpose of this competence element is to enable the individual to contribute to helping societies, organisations and individuals to change or transform their organisation, thereby achieving projected benefits and goals.

Description
From its greater accessibility and approachability, the PMO often plays a connecting role between the project and the people in the organisation in transition. To be relevant in that role, the PMO-er must understand the change process and be able to assess the organisation's adaptability and identify change requirements and transformation opportunities. From that position, the PMO-er can also contribute to the development and implementation of a change or transformation strategy.

Knowledge
- Learning styles for individuals, groups and organisations;
- Organisational change management theories;
- Impact of change on individuals;
- Personal change management techniques;
- Group dynamics;
- Impact analysis;
- Actor analysis;
- Motivation theory;
- Theory of change.

Skills and abilities
- Assessing an individual's, group's or organisation's change capacity and capability;
- Interventions on behaviour of individuals and groups;
- Dealing with resistance to change.

Key competence indicators

Practice 13.1. Assess the adaptability to change of the organisation(s)
- Analyses the adaptability to the required change, based on previous successful and unsuccessful changes in the organisation;
- Assesses possible areas (topics, people) for resistance to the change;

- Recognises and influences circumstances which can improve adaptability;
- Takes action when the required or expected change or transformation is not within the capabilities of the organisation(s).

Practice 13.2. Identify change requirements and transformation opportunities
- Identifies groups and individuals affected by change
- Maps group interests
- Identifies change requirements and opportunities regularly
- Adapts to changing interests and situations

Practice 13.3. Develop change or transformation strategy
- Identifies societal, organisational and personal change or transformation strategies, recognising, for example, innovators, early adopters, the majority and laggards;
- Collaborates with others to validate strategies;
- Documents strategies into a comprehensive change plan;
- Develops a step-by-step approach if this is required;
- Regularly adapts the change or transformation plan to incorporate lessons learned and changes in the project's environment, or in society;
- Regularly adapts the strategy because the change has succeeded and benefits have been achieved.

Practice 13.4. Implement change or transformation management strategy
- Designs a coherent intervention plan;
- Implements selected interventions;
- Leads or organises workshops and training;
- Addresses resistance to change;
- Organises and implements mass media interventions;
- Uses reinforcement techniques to ensure new behaviour is sustainable.

www.ingramcontent.com/pod-product-compliance
Lightning Source LLC
Chambersburg PA
CBHW082111210326
41599CB00033B/6667